Boston, 135 Washington Street,
November, 1850.

NEW BOOKS AND NEW EDITIONS

PUBLISHED BY

Ticknor, Reed, and Fields.

MR. LONGFELLOW'S POEMS.

MR. LONGFELLOW'S COMPLETE POETICAL WORKS. This edition contains the six volumes mentioned below, and is the only complete collection in the market. In two volumes, 16mo, $2.00.

In separate Volumes, each 75 cents.

THE SEASIDE AND THE FIRESIDE.

EVANGELINE; A Tale of Acadie.

VOICES OF THE NIGHT.

BALLADS and OTHER POEMS.

SPANISH STUDENT. A Play in Three Acts.

BELFRY OF BRUGES and OTHER POEMS.

THE WAIF. A Collection of Poems. Edited by Longfellow.

THE ESTRAY. A Collection of Poems. Edited by Longfellow.

MR. LONGFELLOW'S PROSE WORKS.

KAVANAGH. A Tale. Lately Published. In one volume, 16mo, price 75 cents.

OUTRE-MER. A Pilgrimage Beyond the Sea. In one volume, 16mo, price $1.00.

HYPERION. A Romance. In one volume, 16mo, price $1.00.

POETRY.

OLIVER WENDELL HOLMES. Poems. In one volume, 16mo. New Edition, Enlarged, with fine Portrait. Price $1.00.

OLIVER WENDELL HOLMES. Astræa, the Balance of Illusions. Just Published. In one volume, 16mo, price 25 cents.

CHARLES SPRAGUE. Poetical and Prose Writings. New and Revised Edition. With fine Portrait. In one volume, 16mo, price 75 cents.

JAMES RUSSELL LOWELL. Complete Poetical Works. Revised, with Additions. In two volumes 16mo, price $1.50.

JAMES RUSSELL LOWELL. The Nooning. In one volume, 16mo. (Just ready.)

JOHN G. WHITTIER. Songs of Labor and Other Poems. In one volume, 16mo, price 50 cents.

JOHN G. SAXE. Humorous and Satirical Poems. In one volume, 16mo, price 50 cents.

ROBERT BROWNING. Complete Poetical Works. In two volumes, 16mo, price $2.00.

ALFRED TENNYSON. Poems. A New Edition, Enlarged, with Portrait. In two volumes, 16mo, price $1.50.

ALFRED TENNYSON. The Princess. A Medley. Just out. In one volume, 16mo, price 50 cents.

ALFRED TENNYSON. In Memoriam. In one volume, 16mo, price 75 cents.

WILLIAM MOTHERWELL. Poems, Narrative and Lyrical. A New Edition, Enlarged. In one volume, 16mo, price 75 cents.

WILLIAM MOTHERWELL. Minstrelsy, Ancient and Modern. With an HISTORICAL INTRODUCTION and NOTES. In two volumes, 16mo, price $1.50.

RICHARD MONCKTON MILNES. Poems of Many Years. In one volume, 16mo, price 75 cents.

PHILLIP JAMES BAILEY. Author of "Festus." THE ANGEL WORLD AND OTHER POEMS. In one volume, 16mo, price 50 cents.

JAMES T. FIELDS. Poems. A New Edition. In one volume, 16mo, price 50 cents.

GRACE GREENWOOD. Poems. In one volume, 16mo, with fine Portrait. (Just ready.)

MEMORY AND HOPE. A BOOK OF POEMS, REFERRING TO CHILDHOOD. In one volume, 8vo. (Just ready.)

REJECTED ADDRESSES. From the last London Edition. Carefully Revised. With an ORIGINAL PREFACE and NOTES. By HORACE and JAMES SMITH. In one volume, 16mo, price 50 cents.

EACH OF THE ABOVE POEMS AND PROSE WRITINGS, MAY BE HAD IN VARIOUS STYLES OF HANDSOME BINDING.

MISCELLANEOUS.

ALDERBROOK. A Collection of Fanny Forester's VILLAGE SKETCHES, POEMS, etc. In two volumes, 12mo, with a fine Portrait of the Author. A New Edition, Enlarged. Just out. Price $1.75.

GREENWOOD LEAVES. A Collection of GRACE GREENWOOD'S Stories and Letters. In one volume, 12mo. New Edition. Price $1.25.

HISTORY OF MY PETS. A BOOK FOR CHILDREN. By GRACE GREENWOOD. With fine Engravings. (Just ready.)

NATHANIEL HAWTHORNE. THE SCARLET LETTER. A ROMANCE. In one volume, 16mo, price 75 cents.

NATHANIEL HAWTHORNE. TWICE-TOLD TALES. A New Edition. In two volumes, 16mo. (Just ready.)

NATHANIEL HAWTHORNE. TRUE STORIES FROM HISTORY AND BIOGRAPHY. In one volume, 16mo, with fine Engravings. (Just ready.)

HORACE MANN. A FEW THOUGHTS FOR A YOUNG MAN. In one volume, 16mo, price 25 cents.

EDWIN P. WHIPPLE. LECTURES ON SUBJECTS CONNECTED WITH LITERATURE AND LIFE. In one volume, 16mo. Just published. Price 63 cents.

EDWIN P. WHIPPLE. ESSAYS AND REVIEWS. A New and Revised Edition. In two volumes, 16mo. (Just ready.)

EDWIN P. WHIPPLE. WASHINGTON AND THE REVOLUTION. In one volume, 16mo, price 20 cents.

JOHN G. WHITTIER. OLD PORTRAITS AND MODERN SKETCHES. In one volume, 16mo. Just published. Price 75 cents.

JOHN G. WHITTIER. MARGARET SMITH'S JOURNAL. In one volume, 16mo, price 75 cents.

HENRY GILES. LECTURES, ESSAYS, AND MISCELLANEOUS WRITINGS. Two volumes, 16mo, price $1.50.

HENRY GILES. CHRISTIAN THOUGHT ON LIFE. In Twelve Discourses. In one volume, 16mo, price 75 cents.

THE BOSTON BOOK. BEING SPECIMENS OF METROPOLITAN LITERATURE. In one volume, 12mo, price $1.25.

CHARLES SUMNER. ORATIONS AND SPEECHES. In two volumes, 16mo. (Nearly ready.)

HEROINES OF THE MISSIONARY ENTERPRIZE. BEING MEMOIRS OF DISTINGUISHED AMERICAN FEMALE MISSIONARIES. In one volume, 16mo, price 75 cents.

F. W. P. GREENWOOD. SERMONS OF CONSOLATION. A New Edition, on very fine paper and large type. In one volume, 16mo, price $1.00.

CHARACTERISTICS OF WOMEN: MORAL, POETICAL and HISTORICAL. By MRS. JAMESON. New Edition, Corrected and Enlarged. In one volume, 12mo, price $1.00.

THOMAS DE QUINCEY. CONFESSIONS OF AN ENGLISH OPIUM-EATER, &c. In one volume, 16mo, price 75 cents.

THOMAS DE QUINCEY. BIOGRAPHICAL ESSAYS. In one volume, 16mo, price 75 cents.

GOETHE'S WILHELM MEISTER. Translated by CARLYLE. In two volumes, 16mo.. (Just ready.)

GOETHE'S FAUST. Translated by HAYWARD In one volume, 16mo. New Edition. (Just ready.)

ANGEL-VOICES; or WORDS OF COUNSEL FOR OVERCOMING THE WORLD. In one volume, 18mo. A New Edition, Enlarged. Price 38 cents.

THE CONSTITUTION OF MAN; Considered in Relation to External Objects. By GEORGE COMBE. Twenty-seventh American Edition. In one volume, 12mo, price 75 cents.

A PRACTICAL TREATISE ON THE CULTIVATION OF THE GRAPE VINE ON OPEN WALLS. With Plates. In one volume, 12mo, price 62 1-2 cents.

MRS. PUTNAM'S RECEIPT BOOK; AND YOUNG HOUSEKEEPER'S ASSISTANT. A New and Enlarged Edition. In one volume, 16mo, price 50 cents.

LIGHTS AND SHADOWS OF DOMESTIC LIFE In one volume, 16mo, price 62 cents.

SONGS OF LABOR,

AND

OTHER POEMS.

BY

JOHN G. WHITTIER.

BOSTON:
TICKNOR, REED, AND FIELDS.
M DCCC LI.

CAMBRIDGE:
METCALF AND COMPANY,
PRINTERS TO THE UNIVERSITY.

Stereotyped by
HOBART & ROBBINS;
NEW ENGLAND TYPE AND STEREOTYPE FOUNDERY,
BOSTON.

DEDICATION.

I WOULD the gift I offer here
  Might graces from thy favor take,
And, seen through Friendship's atmosphere,
On softened lines and coloring, wear
The unaccustomed light of beauty, for thy sake.

Few leaves of Fancy's spring remain:
  But what I have I give to thee,—
The o'er-sunned bloom of summer's plain,
And paler flowers, the latter rain
Calls from the westering slope of life's autumnal lea.

Above the fallen groves of green,
  Where youth's enchanted forest stood,
The dry and wasting roots between,
A sober after-growth is seen,
As springs the pine where falls the gay-leafed maple wood!

Yet birds will sing, and breezes play
  Their leaf-harps in the sombre tree;
And through the bleak and wintry day
It keeps its steady green alway, —
So, even my after-thoughts may have a charm for thee.

Art's perfect forms no moral need,
  And beauty is its own excuse;[1]
But for the dull and flowerless weed
Some healing virtue still must plead,
And the rough ore must find its honors in its use.

So haply these, my simple lays
  Of homely toil, may serve to show
The orchard bloom and tasselled maize
That skirt and gladden duty's ways,
The unsung beauty hid life's common things below!

Haply from them the toiler, bent
  Above his forge or plough, may gain
A manlier spirit of content,
And feel that life is wisest spent
Where the strong working hand makes strong the working brain: —

The doom which to the guilty pair
  Without the walls of Eden came,
Transforming sinless ease to care
And rugged toil, no more shall bear
The burden of old crime, or mark of primal shame.

A blessing now — a curse no more;
  Since He, whose name we breathe with awe,
The coarse mechanic vesture wore, —
A poor man toiling with the poor,
In labor, as in prayer, fulfilling the same law.

CONTENTS.

SONGS OF LABOR.

PAGE

THE SHIP-BUILDERS, ... 13

THE SHOEMAKERS, ... 18

THE DROVERS, ... 23

THE FISHERMEN, ... 29

THE HUSKERS, ... 34

THE LUMBERMEN, ... 42

POEMS.

PART I.

THE LAKE-SIDE, ... 53

THE HILL-TOP, ... 56

ON RECEIVING AN EAGLE'S QUILL FROM LAKE SUPERIOR, . . . 61

MEMORIES, ... 66

THE LEGEND OF ST. MARK, ... 70

THE WELL OF LOCH MAREE, ... 75

PAGE
TO MY SISTER, ... 77
AUTUMN THOUGHTS, ... 80
CALEF IN BOSTON, 1692, ... 82

PART II.

TO PIUS IX., ... 85
ELLIOTT, ... 90
ICHABOD! 93
THE CHRISTIAN TOURISTS, ... 95
THE MEN OF OLD, ... 99
THE PEACE CONVENTION AT BRUSSELS, ... 103
THE WISH OF TO-DAY, ... 108
OUR STATE, ... 110
EVENING IN BURMAH, ... 112
ALL 'S WELL, ... 117
SEED TIME AND HARVEST, ... 118
TO A. K., ... 120

SONGS OF LABOR.

SONGS OF LABOR.

THE SHIP-BUILDERS.

THE sky is ruddy in the East,
  The earth is gray below,
And, spectral in the river-mist,
  The ship's white timbers show.
Then let the sounds of measured stroke
  And grating saw begin;
The broad-axe to the gnarléd oak,
  The mallet to the pin!

Hark! — roars the bellows, blast on blast,
  The sooty smithy jars,
And fire-sparks, rising far and fast,
  Are fading with the stars.
All day for us the smith shall stand
  Beside that flashing forge;
All day for us his heavy hand
  The groaning anvil scourge.

From far-off hills, the panting team
  For us is toiling near;
For us the raftsmen down the stream
  Their island barges steer.
Rings out for us the axe-man's stroke
  In forests old and still, —
For us the century-circled oak
  Falls crashing down his hill.

Up! — up! — in nobler toil than ours
  No craftsmen bear a part:
We make of Nature's giant powers
  The slaves of human Art.

Lay rib to rib and beam to beam,
  And drive the treenails free;
Nor faithless joint nor yawning seam
  Shall tempt the searching sea!

Where'er the keel of our good ship
  The sea's rough field shall plough—
Where'er her tossing spars shall drip
  With salt-spray caught below—
That ship must heed her master's beck,
  Her helm obey his hand,
And seamen tread her reeling deck
  As if they trod the land.

Her oaken ribs the vulture-beak
  Of Northern ice may peel;
The sunken rock and coral peak
  May grate along her keel;
And know we well the painted shell
  We give to wind and wave,
Must float, the sailor's citadel,
  Or sink, the sailor's grave!

Ho! — strike away the bars and blocks,
And set the good ship free!
Why lingers on these dusty rocks
The young bride of the sea?
Look! how she moves adown the grooves,
In graceful beauty now!
How lowly on the breast she loves
Sinks down her virgin prow!

God bless her! wheresoe'er the breeze
Her snowy wing shall fan,
Aside the frozen Hebrides,
Or sultry Hindostan!
Where'er, in mart or on the main,
With peaceful flag unfurled,
She helps to wind the silken chain
Of commerce round the world!

Speed on the ship! — But let her bear
No merchandise of sin,
No groaning cargo of despair
Her roomy hold within.

No Lethean drug for Eastern lands,
Nor poison-draught for ours;
But honest fruits of toiling hands
And Nature's sun and showers.

Be hers the Prairie's golden grain,
The Desert's golden sand,
The clustered fruits of sunny Spain,
The spice of Morning-land!
Her pathway on the open main
May blessings follow free,
And glad hearts welcome back again
Her white sails from the sea!

2

THE SHOEMAKERS.

Ho! workers of the old time styled
The Gentle Craft of Leather!
Young brothers of the ancient guild,
Stand forth once more together!
Call out again your long array,
In the olden merry manner!
Once more, on gay St. Crispin's day,
Fling out your blazoned banner!

Rap, rap! upon the well-worn stone
How falls the polished hammer!
Rap, rap! the measured sound has grown
A quick and merry clamor.
Now shape the sole! now deftly curl
The glossy vamp around it,
And bless the while the bright-eyed girl
Whose gentle fingers bound it!

For you, along the Spanish main
  A hundred keels are ploughing;
For you, the Indian on the plain
  His lasso-coil is throwing;
For you, deep glens with hemlock dark
  The woodman's fire is lighting;
For you, upon the oak's gray bark,
  The woodman's axe is smiting.

For you, from Carolina's pine
  The rosin-gum is stealing;
For you, the dark-eyed Florentine
  Her silken skein is reeling;
For you, the dizzy goat-herd roams
  His rugged Alpine ledges;
For you, round all her shepherd homes,
  Bloom England's thorny hedges.

The foremost still, by day or night,
  On moated mound or heather,
Where'er the need of trampled right
  Brought toiling men together;

Where the free burghers from the wall
  Defied the mail-clad master,
Than yours, at Freedom's trumpet-call,
  No craftsmen rallied faster.

Let foplings sneer, let fools deride —
  Ye heed no idle scorner;
Free hands and hearts are still your pride,
  And duty done, your honor.
Ye dare to trust, for honest fame,
  The jury Time empanels,
And leave to truth each noble name
  Which glorifies your annals.

Thy songs, Han Sachs, are living yet,
  In strong and hearty German;
And Bloomfield's lay, and Gifford's wit,
  And patriot fame of Sherman;
Still from his book, a mystic seer,
  The soul of Behmen teaches,
And England's priestcraft shakes to hear
  Of Fox's leathern breeches!

The foot is yours; where'er it falls,
  It treads your well-wrought leather,
On earthen floor, in marble halls,
  On carpet, or on heather.
Still there the sweetest charm is found
  Of matron grace or vestal's,
As Hebe's foot bore nectar round
  Among the old celestials!

Rap! rap! — your stout and bluff brogan,
  With footsteps slow and weary,
May wander where the sky's blue span
  Shuts down upon the prairie.
On Beauty's foot, your slippers glance,
  By Saratoga's fountains,
Or twinkle down the summer dance
  Beneath the Crystal Mountains!

The red brick to the mason's hand,
  The brown earth to the tiller's,
The shoe in yours shall wealth command,
  Like fairy Cinderella's!

As they who shunned the household maid
  Beheld the crown upon her,
So all shall see your toil repaid
  With hearth and home and honor.

Then let the toast be freely quaffed,
  In water cool and brimming—
"All honor to the good old Craft,
  Its merry men and women!"
Call out again your long array,
  In the old time's pleasant manner;
Once more, on gay St. Crispin's day,
  Fling out his blazoned banner!

THE DROVERS.

THROUGH heat and cold, and shower and sun,
  Still onward cheerly driving!
There 's life alone in duty done,
  And rest alone in striving.
But see! the day is closing cool,
  The woods are dim before us;
The white fog of the way-side pool
  Is creeping slowly o'er us.

The night is falling, comrades mine,
  Our foot-sore beasts are weary,
And through yon elms the tavern sign
  Looks out upon us cheery.
The landlord beckons from his door,
  His beechen fire is glowing;
These ample barns, with feed in store,
  Are filled to overflowing.

From many a valley frowned across
By brows of rugged mountains;
From hill-sides where, through spongy moss,
Gush out the river fountains;
From quiet farm-fields, green and low,
And bright with blooming clover;
From vales of corn the wandering crow
No richer hovers over;

Day after day our way has been,
O'er many a hill and hollow;
By lake and stream, by wood and glen,
Our stately drove we follow.
Through dust-clouds rising thick and dun,
As smoke of battle o'er us,
Their white horns glisten in the sun,
Like plumes and crests before us.

We see them slowly climb the hill,
As slow behind it sinking;
Or, thronging close, from road-side rill,
Or sunny lakelet, drinking.

Now crowding in the narrow road,
In thick and struggling masses,
They glare upon the teamster's load,
Or rattling coach that passes.

Anon, with toss of horn and tail,
And paw of hoof, and bellow,
They leap some farmer's broken pale,
O'er meadow-close or fallow.
Forth comes the startled good-man; forth
Wife, children, house-dog, sally,
Till once more on their dusty path
The baffled truants rally.

We drive no starvelings, scraggy grown,
Loose-legged, and ribbed and bony,
Like those who grind their noses down
On pastures bare and stony —
Lank oxen, rough as Indian dogs,
And cows too lean for shadows,
Disputing feebly with the frogs
The crop of saw-grass meadows!

In our good drove, so sleek and fair,
No bones of leanness rattle;
No tottering hide-bound ghosts are there,
Or Pharaoh's evil cattle.
Each stately beeve bespeaks the hand
That fed him unrepining;
The fatness of a goodly land
In each dun hide is shining.

We 've sought them where, in warmest nooks,
The freshest feed is growing,
By sweetest springs and clearest brooks
Through honeysuckle flowing;
Wherever hill-sides, sloping south,
Are bright with early grasses,
Or, trackling green the lowland's drouth,
The mountain streamlet passes.

But now the day is closing cool,
The woods are dim before us,
The white fog of the way-side pool
Is creeping slowly o'er us.

The cricket to the frog's bassoon
His shrillest time is keeping;
The sickle of yon setting moon
The meadow-mist is reaping.

The night is falling, comrades mine,
Our foot-sore beasts are weary,
And through yon elms the tavern sign
Looks out upon us cheery.
To-morrow, eastward with our charge
We'll go to meet the dawning,
Ere yet the pines of Kéarsarge
Have seen the sun of morning.

When snow-flakes o'er the frozen earth,
Instead of birds, are flitting;
When children throng the glowing hearth,
And quiet wives are knitting;
While in the fire-light strong and clear
Young eyes of pleasure glisten,
To tales of all we see and hear
The ears of home shall listen.

By many a Northern lake and hill,
  From many a mountain pasture,
Shall Fancy play the Drover still,
  And speed the long night faster.
Then let us on, through shower and sun,
  And heat and cold, be driving;
There's life alone in duty done,
  And rest alone in striving.

THE FISHERMEN.

HURRAH! the seaward breezes
  Sweep down the bay amain;
Heave up, my lads, the anchor!
  Run up the sail again!
Leave to the lubber landsmen
  The rail-car and the steed;
The stars of heaven shall guide us,
  The breath of heaven shall speed.

From the hill-top looks the steeple,
  And the light-house from the sand;
And the scattered pines are waving
  Their farewell from the land.
One glance, my lads, behind us,
  For the homes we leave one sigh,
Ere we take the change and chances
  Of the ocean and the sky.

Now brothers, for the icebergs
  Of frozen Labrador,
Floating spectral in the moonshine,
  Along the low, black shore!
Where like snow the gannet's feathers
  On Brador's rocks are shed,
And the noisy murr are flying,
  Like black scuds, overhead;

Where in mist the rock is hiding,
  And the sharp reef lurks below,
And the white squall smites in summer,
  And the autumn tempests blow;
Where, through gray and rolling vapor,
  From evening unto morn,
A thousand boats are hailing,
  Horn answering unto horn.

Hurrah! for the Red Island,
  With the white cross on its crown!
Hurrah! for Meccatina,
  And its mountains bare and brown!

Where the Caribou's tall antlers
  O'er the dwarf-wood freely toss,
And the footstep of the Mickmack
  Has no sound upon the moss.

There we 'll drop our lines, and gather
  Old Ocean's treasures in,
Where'er the mottled mackerel
  Turns up a steel-dark fin.
The sea 's our field of harvest,
  Its scaly tribes our grain;
We 'll reap the teeming waters
  As at home they reap the plain!

Our wet hands spread the carpet,
  And light the hearth of home;
From our fish, as in the old time,
  The silver coin shall come.
As the demon fled the chamber
  Where the fish of Tobit lay,
So ours from all our dwellings
  Shall frighten Want away.

Though the mist upon our jackets
 In the bitter air congeals,
And our lines wind stiff and slowly
 From off the frozen reels;
Though the fog be dark around us,
 And the storm blow high and loud,
We will whistle down the wild wind,
 And laugh beneath the cloud!

In the darkness as in daylight,
 On the water as on land,
God's eye is looking on us,
 And beneath us is His hand!
Death will find us soon or later,
 On the deck or in the cot;
And we cannot meet him better
 Than in working out our lot.

Hurrah! — hurrah! — the west wind
 Comes freshening down the bay,
The rising sails are filling —
 Give way, my lads, give way!

Leave the coward landsman clinging
  To the dull earth, like a weed —
The stars of heaven shall guide us,
  And the breath of heaven shall speed!

THE HUSKERS.

It was late in mild October, and the long autumnal
rain
Had left the summer harvest-fields all green with grass
again;
The first sharp frosts had fallen, leaving all the wood-
lands gay
With the hues of summer's rainbow, or the meadow-
flowers of May.

Through a thin, dry mist, that morning, the sun rose
broad and red,
At first a rayless disc of fire, he brightened as he sped;
Yet, even his noontide glory fell chastened and sub-
dued,
On the corn-fields and the orchards, and softly pictured
wood.

And all that quiet afternoon, slow sloping to the night,
He wove with golden shuttle the haze with yellow light;
Slanting through the painted beeches, he glorified the hill;
And, beneath it, pond and meadow lay brighter, greener still.

And shouting boys in woodland haunts caught glimpses of that sky,
Flecked by the many-tinted leaves, and laughed, they knew not why;
And school-girls, gay with aster-flowers, beside the meadow brooks,
Mingled the glow of autumn with the sunshine of sweet looks.

From spire and barn, looked westerly the patient weather-cocks;
But even the birches on the hill stood motionless as rocks.

No sound was in the woodlands, save the squirrel's
dropping shell,
And the yellow leaves among the boughs, low rustling
as they fell.

The summer grains were harvested; the stubble-fields
lay dry,
Where June winds rolled, in light and shade, the pale-
green waves of rye;
But still, on gentle hill-slopes, in valleys fringed with
wood,
Ungathered, bleaching in the sun, the heavy corn crop
stood.

Bent low, by autumn's wind and rain, through husks
that, dry and sere,
Unfolded from their ripened charge, shone out the yellow
ear;
Beneath, the turnip lay concealed, in many a verdant
fold,
And glistened in the slanting light the pumpkin's sphere
of gold.

There wrought the busy harvesters; and many a creaking wain
Bore slowly to the long barn-floor its load of husk and grain;
Till broad and red, as when he rose, the sun sank down, at last,
And like a merry guest's farewell, the day in brightness passed.

And lo! as through the western pines, on meadow, stream and pond,
Flamed the red radiance of a sky, set all afire beyond,
Slowly o'er the Eastern sea-bluffs a milder glory shone,
And the sunset and the moonrise were mingled into one!

As thus into the quiet night the twilight lapsed away,
And deeper in the brightening moon the tranquil shadows lay;
From many a brown old farm-house, and hamlet without name,
Their milking and their home-tasks done, the merry huskers came.

Swung o'er the heaped-up harvest, from pitchforks in
the mow,
Shone dimly down the lanterns on the pleasant scene
below;
The growing pile of husks behind, the golden ears before,
And laughing eyes and busy hands and brown cheeks
glimmering o'er.

Half hidden in a quiet nook, serene of look and heart,
Talking their old times over, the old men sat apart;
While, up and down the unhusked pile, or nestling in
its shade,
At hide-and-seek, with laugh and shout, the happy chil-
dren played.

Urged by the good host's daughter, a maiden young and
fair,
Lifting to light her sweet blue eyes and pride of soft
brown hair,
The master of the village school, sleek of hair and
smooth of tongue,
To the quaint tune of some old psalm, a husking-ballad
sung.

THE CORN SONG.

Heap high the farmer's wintry hoard!
  Heap high the golden corn!
No richer gift has Autumn poured
  From out her lavish horn!

Let other lands, exulting, glean
  The apple from the pine,
The orange from its glossy green,
  The cluster from the vine;

We better love the hardy gift
  Our rugged vales bestow,
To cheer us when the storm shall drift
  Our harvest-fields with snow.

Through vales of grass and meads of flowers,
  Our ploughs their furrows made,
While on the hills the sun and showers
  Of changeful April played.

We dropped the seed o'er hill and plain,
  Beneath the sun of May,
And frightened from our sprouting grain
  The robber crows away.

All through the long, bright days of June,
  Its leaves grew green and fair,
And waved in hot midsummer's noon
  Its soft and yellow hair.

And now, with Autumn's moonlit eves,
  Its harvest time has come,
We pluck away the frosted leaves,
  And bear the treasure home.

There, richer than the fabled gift
  Apollo showered of old,
Fair hands the broken grain shall sift,
  And knead its meal of gold.

Let vapid idlers loll in silk,
  Around their costly board;
Give us the bowl of samp and milk,
  By homespun beauty poured!

Where'er the wide old kitchen hearth
  Sends up its smoky curls,
Who will not thank the kindly earth,
  And bless our farmer girls!

Then shame on all the proud and vain,
  Whose folly laughs to scorn
The blessing of our hardy grain,
  Our wealth of golden corn!

Let earth withhold her goodly root,
  Let mildew blight the rye,
Give to the worm the orchard's fruit,
  The wheat-field to the fly:

But let the good old crop adorn
  The hills our fathers trod;
Still let us, for His golden corn,
  Send up our thanks to God!

THE LUMBERMEN.

Wildly round our woodland quarters,
 Sad-voiced Autumn grieves;
Thickly down these swelling waters
 Float his fallen leaves.
Through the tall and naked timber,
 Column-like and old,
Gleam the sunsets of November,
 From their skies of gold.

O'er us, to the southland heading,
 Screams the gray wild-goose;
On the night-frost sounds the treading
 Of the brindled moose.
Noiseless creeping, while we 're sleeping,
 Frost his task-work plies;
Soon, his icy bridges heaping,
 Shall our log-piles rise.

When, with sounds of smothered thunder,
On some night of rain,
Lake and river break asunder
Winter's weakened chain,
Down the wild March flood shall bear them
To the saw-mill's wheel,
Or where Steam, the slave, shall tear them
With his teeth of steel.

Be it starlight, be it moonlight,
In these vales below,
When the earliest beams of sunlight
Streak the mountain's snow,
Crisps the hoar-frost, keen and early,
To our hurrying feet,
And the forest echoes clearly
All our blows repeat.

Where the crystal Ambijejis
Stretches broad and clear,
And Millnoket's pine-black ridges
Hide the browsing deer;

Where, through lakes and wide morasses,
  Or through rocky walls,
Swift and strong, Penobscot passes
  White with foamy falls;

Where, through clouds, are glimpses given
  Of Katahdin's sides, —
Rock and forest piled to heaven,
  Torn and ploughed by slides!
Far below, the Indian trapping,
  In the sunshine warm;
Far above, the snow-cloud wrapping
  Half the peak in storm!

Where are mossy carpets better
  Than the Persian weaves,
And than Eastern perfumes sweeter
  Seem the fading leaves;
And a music wild and solemn,
  From the pine-tree's height,
Rolls its vast and sea-like volume
  On the wind of night;

Make we here our camp of winter;
  And, through sleet and snow,
Pitchy knot and beechen splinter
  On our hearth shall glow.
Here, with mirth to lighten duty,
  We shall lack alone
Woman's smile and girlhood's beauty,
  Childhood's lisping tone.

But their hearth is brighter burning
  For our toil to-day;
And the welcome of returning
  Shall our loss repay,
When, like seamen from the waters,
  From the woods we come,
Greeting sisters, wives and daughters,
  Angels of our home!

Not for us the measured ringing
  From the village spire,
Not for us the Sabbath singing
  Of the sweet-voiced choir:

Ours the old, majestic temple,
  Where God's brightness shines
Down the dome so grand and ample,
  Propped by lofty pines!

Through each branch-enwoven skylight,
  Speaks He in the breeze,
As of old beneath the twilight
  Of lost Eden's trees!
For His ear, the inward feeling
  Needs no outward tongue;
He can see the spirit kneeling
  While the axe is swung.

Heeding truth alone, and turning
  From the false and dim,
Lamp of toil or altar burning
  Are alike to Him.
Strike, then, comrades! — Trade is waiting
  On our rugged toil;
Far ships waiting for the freighting
  Of our woodland spoil!

Ships, whose traffic links these highlands,
  Bleak and cold, of ours,
With the citron-planted islands
  Of a clime of flowers;
To our frosts the tribute bringing
  Of eternal heats;
In our lap of winter flinging
  Tropic fruits and sweets.

Cheerly, on the axe of labor,
  Let the sunbeams dance,
Better than the flash of sabre
  Or the gleam of lance!
Strike! — With every blow is given
  Freer sun and sky,
And the long-hid earth to heaven
  Looks, with wondering eye!

Loud behind us grow the murmurs
  Of the age to come;
Clang of smiths, and tread of farmers,
  Bearing harvest home!

Here her virgin lap with treasures
  Shall the green earth fill;
Waving wheat and golden maize-ears
  Crown each beechen hill.

Keep who will the city's alleys,
  Take the smooth-shorn plain, —
Give to us the cedar valleys,
  Rocks and hills of Maine!
In our North-land, wild and woody,
  Let us still have part;
Rugged nurse and mother sturdy,
  Hold us to thy heart!

O! our free hearts beat the warmer
  For thy breath of snow;
And our tread is all the firmer
  For thy rocks below.
Freedom, hand in hand with labor,
  Walketh strong and brave;
On the forehead of his neighbor
  No man writeth Slave!

Lo, the day breaks! old Katahdin's
  Pine-trees show its fires,
While from these dim forest gardens
  Rise their blackened spires.
Up, my comrades! up and doing!
  Manhood's rugged play
Still renewing, bravely hewing
  Through the world our way!

POEMS.

POEMS.

PART I.

THE LAKE-SIDE.

THE shadows round the inland sea
  Are deepening into night;
Slow up the slopes of Ossipee
  They chase the lessening light.
Tired of the long day's blinding heat,
  I rest my languid eye,
Lake of the Hills! where, cool and sweet,
  Thy sunset waters lie!

Along the sky, in wavy lines,
  O'er isle and reach and bay,
Green-belted with eternal pines,
  The mountains stretch away.

Below, the maple masses sleep
  Where shore with water blends,
While midway on the tranquil deep
  The evening light descends.

So seemed it when yon hill's red crown,
  Of old, the Indian trod,
And, through the sunset air, looked down
  Upon the Smile of God.[2]
To him, of light and shade the laws
  No forest sceptic taught;
Their living and eternal Cause
  His truer instinct sought.

He saw these mountains in the light
  Which now across them shines;
This lake, in summer sunset bright,
  Walled round with sombering pines.
God near him seemed; from earth and skies
  His loving voice he heard,
As, face to face, in Paradise,
  Man stood before the Lord.

Thanks, oh, our Father! that, like him,
  Thy tender love I see,
In radiant hill and woodland dim,
  And tinted sunset sea.
For not in mockery dost Thou fill
  Our earth with light and grace;
Thou hid'st no dark and cruel will
  Behind Thy smiling face!

THE HILL-TOP.

The burly driver at my side,
  We slowly climbed the hill,
Whose summit, in the hot noontide,
  Seemed rising, rising still.
At last, our short noon-shadows hid
  The top-stone, bare and brown,
From whence, like Gizeh's pyramid,
  The rough mass slanted down.

I felt the cool breath of the North;
  Between me and the sun,
O'er deep, still lake, and ridgy earth,
  I saw the cloud-shades run.
Before me, stretched for glistening miles,
  Lay mountain-girdled Squam;
Like green-winged birds, the leafy isles
  Upon its bosom swam.

And, glimmering through the sun-haze warm,
  Far as the eye could roam,
Dark billows of an earthquake storm
  Beflecked with clouds like foam,
Their vales in misty shadow deep,
  Their rugged peaks in shine,
I saw the mountain ranges sweep
  The horizon's northern line.

There towered Chocorua's peak; and west,
  Moosehillock's woods were seen,
With many a nameless slide-scarred crest
  And pine-dark gorge between.
Beyond them, like a sun-rimmed cloud,
  The great Notch mountains shone,
Watched over by the solemn-browed
  And awful face of stone!

"A good look-off!" the driver spake:
  "About this time, last year,
I drove a party to the Lake,
  And stopped, at evening, here.

'T was duskish down below; but all
These hills stood in the sun,
Till, dipped behind yon purple wall,
He left them, one by one.

"A lady, who, from Thornton hill,
Had held her place outside,
And, as a pleasant woman will,
Had cheered the long, dull ride,
Besought me, with so sweet a smile,
That — though I hate delays —
I could not choose but rest awhile —
(These women have such ways!)

"On yonder mossy ledge she sat,
Her sketch upon her knees,
A stray brown lock beneath her hat
Unrolling in the breeze;
Her sweet face, in the sunset light
Upraised and glorified, —
I never saw a prettier sight
In all my mountain ride.

"As good as fair; it seemed her joy
To comfort and to give;
My poor, sick wife, and cripple boy,
Will bless her while they live!"
The tremor in the driver's tone
His manhood did not shame:
"I dare say, sir, you may have known —"
He named a well-known name.

Then sank the pyramidal mounds,
The blue lake fled away;
For mountain-scope a parlor's bounds,
A lighted hearth for day!
And lonely years and weary miles
Did at that name depart;
Kind voices cheered, sweet human smiles
Shone warm into my heart.

We journeyed on; but earth and sky
Had power to charm no more;
Still dreamed my inward-turning eye
The dream of memory o'er.

Ah! human kindness, human love—
  To few who seek denied—
Too late we learn to prize above
  The whole round world beside!

ON RECEIVING AN EAGLE'S QUILL FROM LAKE SUPERIOR.

All day the darkness and the cold
  Upon my heart have lain,
Like shadows on the winter sky,
  Like frost upon the pane;

But now my torpid fancy wakes,
  And, on thy Eagle's plume,
Rides forth, like Sinbad on his bird,
  Or witch upon her broom!

Below me roar the rocking pines,
  Before me spreads the lake,
Whose long and solemn-sounding waves
  Against the sunset break.

I hear the wild Rice-Eater thresh
  The grain he has not sown;
I see, with flashing scythe of fire,
  The prairie harvest mown!

I hear the far-off voyager's horn;
  I see the Yankee's trail —
His foot on every mountain-pass,
  On every stream his sail.

By forest, lake and water-fall,
  I see his pedler show;
The mighty mingling with the mean,
  The lofty with the low.

He 's whittling by St. Mary's Falls,
  Upon his loaded wain;
He 's measuring o'er the Pictured Rocks,
  With eager eyes of gain.

I hear the mattock in the mine,
  The axe-stroke in the dell,
The clamor from the Indian lodge,
  The Jesuit chapel bell!

I see the swarthy trappers come
  From Mississippi's springs;
And war-chiefs, with their painted brows,
  And crests of eagle wings.

Behind the scared squaw's birch canoe,
The steamer smokes and raves;
And city lots are staked for sale
Above old Indian graves.

I hear the tread of pioneers
Of nations yet to be;
The first low wash of waves, where soon
Shall roll a human sea.

The rudiments of empire here
Are plastic yet, and warm;
The chaos of a mighty world
Is rounding into form!

Each rude and jostling fragment soon
Its fitting place shall find—
The raw material of a State,
Its muscle and its mind!

And, westering still, the star which leads
The New World in its train
Has tipped with fire the icy spears
Of many a mountain chain.

The snowy cones of Oregon
  Are kindling on its way;
And California's golden sands
  Gleam brighter in its ray!

Then, blessings on thy eagle quill,
  As, wandering far and wide,
I thank thee for this twilight dream
  And Fancy's airy ride!

Yet, welcomer than regal plumes,
  Which Western trappers find,
Thy free and pleasant thoughts, chance-sown,
  Like feathers on the wind.

Thy symbol be the mountain-bird,
  Whose glistening quill I hold;
Thy home the ample air of hope,
  And memory's sunset gold!

In thee, let joy with duty join,
  And strength unite with love,
The eagle's pinions folding round
  The warm heart of the dove!

So, when in darkness sleeps the vale
  Where still the blind bird clings,
The sunshine of the upper sky
  Shall glitter on thy wings!

MEMORIES.

A beautiful and happy girl,
  With step as light as summer air,
Eyes glad with smiles, and brow of pearl,
Shadowed by many a careless curl
  Of unconfined and flowing hair:
A seeming child in everything,
  Save thoughtful brow and ripening charms,
As Nature wears the smile of Spring
  When sinking into Summer's arms.

A mind rejoicing in the light
  Which melted through its graceful bower,
Leaf after leaf, dew-moist and bright,
And stainless in its holy white,
  Unfolding like a morning flower:
A heart, which, like a fine-toned lute,
  With every breath of feeling woke,
And, even when the tongue was mute,
  From eye and lip in music spoke.

How thrills once more the lengthening chain
  Of memory, at the thought of thee!
Old hopes which long in dust have lain,
Old dreams, come thronging back again,
  And boyhood lives again in me;
I feel its glow upon my cheek,
  Its fulness of the heart is mine,
As when I leaned to hear thee speak,
  Or raised my doubtful eye to thine.

I hear again thy low replies,
  I feel thy arm within my own,
And timidly again uprise
The fringéd lids of hazel eyes,
  With soft brown tresses overblown.
Ah! memories of sweet summer eves,
  Of moonlit wave and willowy way,
Of stars and flowers, and dewy leaves,
  And smiles and tones more dear than they!

Ere this, thy quiet eye hath smiled
  My picture of thy youth to see,

When, half a woman, half a child,
Thy very artlessness beguiled,
  And folly's self seemed wise in thee;
I too can smile, when o'er that hour
  The lights of memory backward stream,
Yet feel the while that manhood's power
  Is vainer than my boyhood's dream.

Years have passed on, and left their trace
  Of graver care and deeper thought;
And unto me the calm, cold face
Of manhood, and to thee the grace
  Of woman's pensive beauty brought.
More wide, perchance, for blame than praise,
  The school-boy's humble name has flown;
Thine, in the green and quiet ways
  Of unobtrusive goodness known.

And wider yet in thought and deed
  Diverge our pathways, one in youth;
Thine the Genevan's sternest creed,
While answers to my spirit's need
  The Derby dalesman's simple truth.

For thee, the priestly rite and prayer,
  And holy day, and solemn psalm;
For me, the silent reverence where
  My brethren gather, slow and calm.

Yet hath thy spirit left on me
  An impress Time has worn not out,
And something of myself in thee,
A shadow from the past, I see,
  Lingering, even yet, thy way about;
Not wholly can the heart unlearn
  That lesson of its better hours,
Not yet has Time's dull footstep worn
  To common dust that path of flowers.

Thus, while at times before our eyes
  The shadows melt, and fall apart,
And, smiling through them, round us lies
The warm light of our morning skies —
  The Indian Summer of the heart! —
In secret sympathies of mind,
  In founts of feeling which retain
Their pure, fresh flow, we yet may find
  Our early dreams not wholly vain '

THE LEGEND OF ST. MARK.[3]

THE day is closing dark and cold,
  With roaring blast and sleety showers;
And through the dusk the lilacs wear
  The bloom of snow, instead of flowers.

I turn me from the gloom without,
  To ponder o'er a tale of old,
A legend of the age of Faith,
  By dreaming monk or abbess told.

On Tintoretto's canvass lives
  That fancy of a loving heart,
In graceful lines and shapes of power,
  And hues immortal as his art.

In Provence (so the story runs)
  There lived a lord, to whom, as slave,
A peasant boy of tender years
  The chance of trade or conquest gave.

Forth-looking from the castle tower,
  Beyond the hills with almonds dark,
The straining eye could scarce discern
  The chapel of the good St. Mark.

And there, when bitter word or fare
  The service of the youth repaid,
By stealth, before that holy shrine,
  For grace to bear his wrong, he prayed.

The steed stamped at the castle gate,
  The boar-hunt sounded on the hill;
Why staid the Baron from the chase,
  With looks so stern, and words so ill?

"Go, bind yon slave! and let him learn,
  By scathe of fire and strain of cord,
How ill they speed who give dead saints
  The homage due their living lord!"

They bound him on the fearful rack,
  When, through the dungeon's vaulted dark,
He saw the light of shining robes,
  And knew the face of good St. Mark.

Then sank the iron rack apart,
  The cords released their cruel clasp,
The pincers, with their teeth of fire,
  Fell broken from the torturer's grasp.

And lo! before the Youth and Saint,
  Barred door and wall of stone gave way;
And up from bondage and the night
  They passed to freedom and the day!

O, dreaming monk! thy tale is true;—
  O, painter! true thy pencil's art;
In tones of hope and prophecy,
  Ye whisper to my listening heart!

Unheard no burdened heart's appeal
  Moans up to God's inclining ear;
Unheeded by His tender eye,
  Falls to the earth no sufferer's tear.

For still the Lord alone is God!
  The pomp and power of tyrant man
Are scattered at his lightest breath,
  Like chaff before the winnower's fan.

Not always shall the slave uplift
  His heavy hands to Heaven in vain;
God's angel, like the good St. Mark,
  Comes shining down to break his chain!

O, weary ones! ye may not see
  Your helpers in their downward flight;
Nor hear the sound of silver wings
  Slow beating through the hush of night!

But not the less gray Dothan shone,
  With sunbright watchers bending low,
That Fear's dim eye beheld alone
  The spear-heads of the Syrian foe.

There are, who, like the Seer of old,
  Can see the helpers God has sent,
And how life's rugged mountain-side
  Is white with many an angel tent!

They hear the heralds whom our Lord
  Sends down his pathway to prepare;
And light, from others hidden, shines
  On their high place of faith and prayer.

Let such, for earth's despairing ones,
  Hopeless, yet longing to be free,
Breathe once again the Prophet's prayer:
  "Lord, ope their eyes, that they may see!"

THE WELL OF LOCH MAREE.[4]

CALM on the breast of Loch Maree
  A little isle reposes;
A shadow woven of the oak
  And willow o'er it closes.

Within, a Druid's mound is seen,
  Set round with stony warders;
A fountain, gushing through the turf,
  Flows o'er its grassy borders.

And whoso bathes therein his brow,
  With care or madness burning,
Feels once again his healthful thought
  And sense of peace returning.

O! restless heart and fevered brain,
  Unquiet and unstable,
That holy well of Loch Maree
  Is more than idle fable!

Life's changes vex, its discords stun,
  Its glaring sunshine blindeth,
And blest is he who on his way
  That fount of healing findeth!

The shadows of a humbled will
  And contrite heart are o'er it:
Go read its legend — "TRUST IN GOD" —
  On Faith's white stones before it.

TO MY SISTER:

WITH A COPY OF "SUPERNATURALISM OF NEW ENGLAND."

DEAR SISTER! — while the wise and sage
Turn coldly from my playful page,
And count it strange that ripened age
  Should stoop to boyhood's folly;
I know that thou wilt judge aright
Of all which makes the heart more light,
Or lends one star-gleam to the night
  Of clouded Melancholy.

Away with weary cares and themes! —
Swing wide the moon-lit gate of dreams!
Leave free once more the land which teems
  With wonders and romances!
Where thou, with clear discerning eyes,
Shalt rightly read the truth which lies
Beneath the quaintly masking guise
  Of wild and wizard fancies.

Lo! once again our feet we set
On still green wood-paths, twilight wet,
By lonely brooks, whose waters fret
  The roots of spectral beeches;
Again the hearth-fire glimmers o'er
Home's white-washed wall and painted floor,
And young eyes widening to the lore
  Of faery-folks and witches.

Dear heart! — the legend is not vain
Which lights that holy hearth again,
And, calling back from care and pain,
  And death's funereal sadness,
Draws round its old familiar blaze
The clustering groups of happier days,
And lends to sober manhood's gaze
  A glimpse of childish gladness.

And, knowing how my life hath been
A weary work of tongue and pen,
A long, harsh strife, with strong-willed men,
  Thou wilt not chide my turning,

To con, at times, an idle rhyme,
To pluck a flower from childhood's clime,
Or listen, at Life's noon-day chime,
For the sweet bells of Morning!

AUTUMN THOUGHTS.

FROM "MARGARET SMITH'S JOURNAL."

Gone hath the Spring, with all its flowers,
And gone the Summer's pomp and show,
And Autumn, in his leafless bowers,
Is waiting for the Winter's snow.

I said to Earth, so cold and gray,
"An emblem of myself thou art:"
"Not so," the Earth did seem to say,
"For Spring shall warm my frozen heart."

I soothe my wintry sleep with dreams
Of warmer sun and softer rain,
And wait to hear the sound of streams
And songs of merry birds again.

But thou, from whom the Spring hath gone,
For whom the flowers no longer blow,
Who standest blighted and forlorn,
Like Autumn waiting for the snow:

No hope is thine of sunnier hours,
Thy Winter shall no more depart;
No Spring revive thy wasted flowers,
Nor Summer warm thy frozen heart.

CALEF IN BOSTON, 1692.

In the solemn days of old,
  Two men met in Boston town —
One a tradesman frank and bold,
  One a preacher of renown.

Cried the last, in bitter tone —
  "Poisoner of the wells of truth!
Satan's hireling, thou hast sown
  With his tares the heart of youth!"

Spake the simple tradesman then —
  "God be judge 'twixt thou and I;
All thou knowest of truth hath been
  Unto men like thee a lie.

"Falsehoods which we spurn to-day
  Were the truths of long ago;
Let the dead boughs fall away,
  Fresher shall the living grow.

" God is good and God is light,
  In this faith I rest secure;
Evil can but serve the right,
  Over all shall love endure.

" Of your spectral puppet play
  I have traced the cunning wires;
Come what will, I needs must say,
  God is true, and ye are liars."

When the thought of man is free,
  Error fears its lightest tones;
So the priest cried, " Sadducee! "
  And the people took up stones.

In the ancient burying-ground,
  Side by side the twain now lie —
One with humble grassy mound,
  One with marbles pale and high.

But the Lord hath blest the seed
  Which that tradesman scattered then,
And the preacher's spectral creed
  Chills no more the blood of men.

Let us trust, to one is known
  Perfect love which casts out fear,
While the other's joys atone
  For the wrong he suffered here.

PART II.

TO PIUS IX.[5]

THE cannon's brazen lips are cold;
No red shell blazes down the air;
And street and tower, and temple old,
Are silent as despair.

The Lombard stands no more at bay —
Rome's fresh young life has bled in vain;
The ravens scattered by the day
Come back with night again.

Now, while the fratricides of France
Are treading on the neck of Rome,
Hider at Gaeta — seize thy chance!
Coward and cruel, come!

Creep now from Naples' bloody skirt;
 Thy mummer's part was acted well,
While Rome, with steel and fire begirt,
 Before thy crusade fell!

Her death-groans answered to thy prayer;
 Thy chant, the drum and bugle-call;
Thy lights, the burning villa's glare;
 Thy beads, the shell and ball!

Let Austria clear thy way, with hands
 Foul from Ancona's cruel sack,
And Naples, with his dastard bands
 Of murderers, lead thee back!

Rome's lips are dumb; the orphan's wail,
 The mother's shriek, thou may'st not hear,
Above the faithless Frenchman's hail,
 The unsexed shaveling's cheer!

Go, bind on Rome her cast-off weight,
 The double curse of crook and crown,
Though woman's scorn and manhood's hate
 From wall and roof flash down!

Nor heed those blood-stains on the wall,
  Not Tiber's flood can wash away,
Where, in thy stately Quirinal,
  Thy mangled victims lay!

Let the world murmur; let its cry
  Of horror and disgust be heard;—
Truth stands alone; thy coward lie
  Is backed by lance and sword!

The cannon of St. Angelo,
  And chanting priest and clanging bell,
And beat of drum and bugle blow,
  Shall greet thy coming well!

Let lips of iron and tongues of slaves
  Fit welcome give thee;—for her part,
Rome, frowning o'er her new-made graves,
  Shall curse thee from her heart!

No wreaths of sad Campagna's flowers
  Shall childhood in thy pathway fling;
No garlands from their ravaged bowers
  Shall Terni's maidens bring;

But, hateful as that tyrant old,
The mocking witness of his crime,
In thee shall loathing eyes behold
The Nero of our time!

Stand where Rome's blood was freest shed,
Mock Heaven with impious thanks, and call
Its curses on the patriot dead,
Its blessings on the Gaul!

Or sit upon thy throne of lies,
A poor, mean idol, blood-besmeared,
Whom even its worshippers despise —
Unhonored, unrevered!

Yet, Scandal of the World! from thee
One needful truth mankind shall learn —
That kings and priests to Liberty
And God are false in turn.

Earth wearies of them; and the long
Meek sufferance of the Heavens doth fail;
Woe for weak tyrants, when the strong
Wake, struggle and prevail!

Not vainly Roman hearts have bled
  To feed the Crozier and the Crown,
If, roused thereby, the world shall tread
  The twin-born vampires down!

ELLIOTT.[6]

HANDS off! thou tythe-fat plunderer! play
  No trick of priestcraft here!
Back, puny lordling! darest thou lay
  A hand on Elliott's bier?
Alive, your rank and pomp, as dust,
  Beneath his feet he trod:
He knew the locust swarm that cursed
  The harvest-fields of God.

On these pale lips, the smothered thought
  Which England's millions feel,
A fierce and fearful splendor caught,
  As from his forge the steel.
Strong-armed as Thor — a shower of fire
  His smitten anvil flung;
God's curse, Earth's wrong, dumb Hunger's ire —
  He gave them all a tongue!

Then let the poor man's horny hands
  Bear up the mighty dead,
And labor's swart and stalwart bands
  Behind as mourners tread.
Leave cant and craft their baptized bounds,
  Leave rank its minster floor;
Give England's green and daisied grounds
  The poet of the poor!

Lay down upon his Sheaf's green verge
  That brave old heart of oak,
With fitting dirge from sounding forge,
  And pall of furnace smoke!
Where whirls the stone its dizzy rounds,
  And axe and sledge are swung,
And, timing to their stormy sounds,
  His stormy lays are sung.

There let the peasant's step be heard,
  The grinder chant his rhyme;
Nor patron's praise nor dainty word
  Befits the man or time.

No soft lament nor dreamer's sigh
For him whose words were bread —
The Runic rhyme and spell whereby
The foodless poor were fed!

Pile up thy tombs of rank and pride,
O England, as thou wilt!
With pomp to nameless worth denied,
Emblazon titled guilt!
No part or lot in these we claim;
But, o'er the sounding wave,
A common right to Elliott's name,
A freehold in his grave!

ICHABOD!

So fallen! so lost! the light withdrawn
Which once he wore!
The glory from his gray hairs gone
Forevermore!

Revile him not — the Tempter hath
A snare for all;
And pitying tears, not scorn and wrath,
Befit his fall!

Oh! dumb be passion's stormy rage,
When he who might
Have lighted up and led his age,
Falls back in night.

Scorn! would the angels laugh, to mark
A bright soul driven,
Fiend-goaded, down the endless dark,
From hope and heaven!

Let not the land, once proud of him,
    Insult him now,
Nor brand with deeper shame his dim,
    Dishonored brow.

But let its humbled sons, instead,
    From sea to lake,
A long lament, as for the dead,
    In sadness make.

Of all we loved and honored, nought
    Save power remains —
A fallen angel's pride of thought,
    Still strong in chains.

All else is gone; from those great eyes
    The soul has fled:
When faith is lost, when honor dies,
    The man is dead!

Then, pay the reverence of old days
    To his dead fame;
Walk backward, with averted gaze,
    And hide the shame!

THE CHRISTIAN TOURISTS.[7]

No aimless wanderers, by the fiend Unrest
Goaded from shore to shore;
No schoolmen, turning, in their classic quest,
The leaves of empire o'er.
Simple of faith, and bearing in their hearts
The love of man and God,
Isles of old song, the Moslem's ancient marts,
And Scythia's steppes, they trod.

Where the long shadows of the fir and pine
In the night sun are cast,
And the deep heart of many a Norland mine
Quakes at each riving blast;
Where, in barbaric grandeur, Moskwa stands,
A baptized Scythian queen,
With Europe's arts and Asia's jewelled hands,
The North and East between!

Where still, through vales of Grecian fable, stray
    The classic forms of yore,
And Beauty smiles, new risen from the spray,
    And Dian weeps once more;
Where every tongue in Smyrna's mart resounds;
    And Stamboul from the sea
Lifts her tall minarets over burial-grounds
    Black with the cypress tree!

From Malta's temples to the gates of Rome,
    Following the track of Paul,
And where the Alps gird round the Switzer's home
    Their vast, eternal wall;
They paused not by the ruins of old time,
    They scanned no pictures rare,
Nor lingered where the snow-locked mountains climb
    The cold abyss of air!

But unto prisons, where men lay in chains,
    To haunts where Hunger pined,
To kings and courts forgetful of the pains
    And wants of human kind,

Scattering sweet words, and quiet deeds of good,
    Along their way, like flowers,
Or, pleading as Christ's freemen only could,
    With princes and with powers;

Their single aim the purpose to fulfil
    Of Truth, from day to day,
Simply obedient to its guiding will,
    They held their pilgrim way.
Yet dream not, hence, the beautiful and old
    Were wasted on their sight,
Who in the school of Christ had learned to hold
    All outward things aright.

Not less to them the breath of vineyards blown
    From off the Cyprian shore,
Not less for them the Alps in sunset shone,
    That man they valued more.
A life of beauty lends to all it sees
    The beauty of its thought;
And fairest forms and sweetest harmonies
    Make glad its way, unsought.

In sweet accordancy of praise and love,
The singing waters run;
And sunset mountains wear in light above
The smile of duty done;
Sure stands the promise — ever to the meek
A heritage is given;
Nor lose they Earth who, single-hearted, seek
The righteousness of Heaven !

THE MEN OF OLD.

WELL speed thy mission, bold Iconoclast!
  Yet all unworthy of its trust thou art,
  If, with dry eye, and cold, unloving heart,
Thou tread'st the solemn Pantheon of the Past,
  By the great Future's dazzling hope made blind
  To all the beauty, power, and truth, behind.
Not without reverent awe shouldst thou put by
  The cypress branches and the amaranth blooms,
  Where, with clasped hands of prayer, upon their tombs
The effigies of old confessors lie,
God's witnesses; the voices of His will,
Heard in the slow march of the centuries still!
Such were the men at whose rebuking frown,
Dark with God's wrath, the tyrant's knee went down;
Such from the terrors of the guilty drew
The vassal's freedom and the poor man's due.

St. Anselm (may he rest forevermore
In Heaven's sweet peace!) forbade, of old, the sale
Of men as slaves, and from the sacred pale
Hurled the Northumbrian buyers of the poor.
To ransom souls from bonds and evil fate,
St. Ambrose melted down the sacred plate —
Image of saint, the chalice and the pix,
Crosses of gold, and silver candlesticks.
"MAN IS WORTH MORE THAN TEMPLES!" he replied
To such as came his holy work to chide.
And brave Cesarius, stripping altars bare,
And coining from the Abbey's golden hoard
The captive's freedom, answered to the prayer
Or threat of those whose fierce zeal for the Lord
Stifled their love of man — "An earthen dish
The last sad supper of the Master bore:
Most miserable sinners! do ye wish
More than your Lord, and grudge His dying poor
What your own pride and not His need requires?
Souls, than these shining gauds, He values more;
Mercy, not sacrifice, His heart desires!"

O faithful worthies! resting far behind
In your dark ages, since ye fell asleep,
Much has been done for truth and human kind —
Shadows are scattered wherein ye groped blind;
Man claims his birthright, freer pulses leap
Through peoples driven in your day like sheep;
Yet, like your own, our age's sphere of light,
Though widening still, is walled around by night;
With slow, reluctant eye, the Church has read,
Sceptic at heart, the lessons of its Head;
Counting, too oft, its living members less
Than the wall's garnish and the pulpit's dress;
World-moving zeal, with power to bless and feed
Life's fainting pilgrims, to their utter need,
Instead of bread, holds out the stone of creed;
Sect builds and worships where its wealth and pride
And vanity stand shrined and deified,
Careless that in the shadow of its walls
God's living temple into ruin falls.
We need, methinks, the prophet-hero still,
Saints true of life, and martyrs strong of will,

To tread the land, even now, as Xavier trod
  The streets of Goa, barefoot, with his bell,
Proclaiming freedom in the name of God,
  And startling tyrants with the fear of hell!
  Soft words, smooth prophecies, are doubtless well;
But to rebuke the age's popular crime,
We need the souls of fire, the hearts of that old time!

THE PEACE CONVENTION AT BRUSSELS.

Still in thy streets, oh Paris! doth the stain
Of blood defy the cleansing autumn rain;
Still breaks the smoke Messina's ruins through,
And Naples mourns that new Bartholomew,
When squalid beggary, for a dole of bread,
At a crowned murderer's beck of license fed
The yawning trenches with her noble dead;
Still, doomed Vienna, through thy stately halls
The shell goes crashing and the red shot falls,
And, leagued to crush thee, on the Danube's side,
The bearded Croat and Bosniak spearman ride;
Still in that vale where Himalaya's snow
Melts round the cornfields and the vines below,
The Sikh's hot cannon, answering ball for ball,
Flames in the breach of Moultan's shattered wall;
On Chenab's side the vulture seeks the slain,
And Sutlej paints with blood its banks again.

"What folly, then," the faithless critic cries,
With sneering lip, and wise, world-knowing eyes,
"While fort to fort, and post to post, repeat
The ceaseless challenge of the war-drum's beat,
And round the green earth, to the church-bell's chime,
The morning drum-roll of the camp keeps time,
To dream of peace amidst a world in arms,
Of swords to ploughshares changed by scriptural charms,
Of nations, drunken with the wine of blood,
Staggering to take the Pledge of Brotherhood,
Like tipplers answering Father Mathew's call —
The sullen Spaniard, and the mad-cap Gaul,
The bull-dog Briton, yielding but with life,
The Yankee swaggering with his bowie knife,
The Russ, from banquets with the vulture shared,
The blood still dripping from his amber beard,
Quitting their mad Berserker dance, to hear
The dull, meek droning of a drab-coat seer;
Leaving the sport of Presidents and Kings,
Where men for dice each titled gambler flings,
To meet alternate on the Seine and Thames,
For tea and gossip, like old country dames!

No! let the cravens plead the weakling's cant,
Let Cobden cipher, and let Vincent rant,
Let Sturge preach peace to democratic throngs,
And Burritt, stammering through his hundred tongues,
Repeat, in all, his ghostly lessons o'er,
Timed to the pauses of the battery's roar;
Check Ban or Kaiser with the barricade
Of "Olive-leaves" and Resolutions made,
Spike guns with pointed scripture-texts, and hope
To capsize navies with a windy trope;
Still shall the glory and the pomp of War
Along their train the shouting millions draw;
Still dusty Labor to the passing Brave
His cap shall doff, and Beauty's kerchief wave;
Still shall the bard to Valor tune his song,
Still Hero-worship kneel before the Strong;
Rosy and sleek, the sable-gowned divine,
O'er his third bottle of suggestive wine,
To plumed and sworded auditors, shall prove
Their trade accordant with the Law of Love;
And Church for State, and State for Church, shall fight,
And both agree, that Might alone is Right!"

Despite of sneers like these, oh, faithful few,
Who dare to hold God's word and witness true,
Whose clear-eyed faith transcends our evil time,
And, o'er the present wilderness of crime,
Sees the calm future, with its robes of green,
Its fleece-flecked mountains, and soft streams between, —
Still keep the path which duty bids ye tread,
Though worldly wisdom shake the cautious head;
No truth from Heaven descends upon our sphere,
Without the greeting of the sceptic's sneer;
Denied, and mocked at, till its blessings fall,
Common as dew and sunshine, over all.

Then, o'er Earth's war-field, till the strife shall cease,
Like Morven's harpers, sing your song of peace;
As in old fable rang the Thracian's lyre,
Midst howl of fiends and roar of penal fire,
Till the fierce din to pleasing murmurs fell,
And love subdued the maddened heart of hell.
Lend, once again, that holy song a tongue,
Which the glad angels of the Advent sung,
Their cradle-anthem for the Saviour's birth,
Glory to God, and peace unto the earth!

Through the mad discord send that calming word
Which wind and wave on wild Genesereth heard,
Lift in Christ's name His Cross against the Sword!
Not vain the vision which the prophets saw,
Skirting with green the fiery waste of war,
Through the hot sand-gleam, looming soft and calm
On the sky's rim, the fountain-shading palm.
Still lives for Earth, which fiends so long have trod,
The great hope resting on the truth of God —
Evil shall cease and Violence pass away,
And the tired world breathe free through a long Sabbath
day.

11*th Mo.*, 1848.

THE WISH OF TO-DAY.

I ASK not now for gold to gild
  With mocking shine a weary frame;
The yearning of the mind is stilled —
  I ask not now for Fame.

A rose-cloud, dimly seen above,
  Melting in heaven's blue depths away —
O! sweet, fond dream of human Love!
  For thee I may not pray.

But, bowed in lowliness of mind,
  I make my humble wishes known —
I only ask a will resigned,
  O, Father, to thine own!

To-day, beneath thy chastening eye,
  I crave alone for peace and rest,
Submissive in thy hand to lie,
  And feel that it is best.

A marvel seems the Universe,
  A miracle our Life and Death;
A mystery which I cannot pierce,
  Around, above, beneath,

In vain I task my aching brain,
  In vain the sage's thought I scan;
I only feel how weak and vain,
  How poor and blind, is man.

And now my spirit sighs for home,
  And longs for light whereby to see,
And, like a weary child, would come,
  O, Father, unto Thee!

Though oft, like letters traced on sand,
  My weak resolves have passed away,
In mercy lend thy helping hand
  Unto my prayer to-day!

OUR STATE.

THE South-land boasts its teeming cane,
The prairied West its heavy grain,
And sunset's radiant gates unfold
On rising marts and sands of gold!

Rough, bleak and hard, our little State
Is scant of soil, of limits strait;
Her yellow sands are sands alone,
Her only mines are ice and stone!

From Autumn frost to April rain,
Too long her winter woods complain;
From budding flower to falling leaf,
Her summer time is all too brief.

Yet, on her rocks, and on her sands,
And wintry hills, the school-house stands,
And what her rugged soil denies,
The harvest of the mind supplies.

The riches of the commonwealth
Are free, strong minds, and hearts of health;
And more to her than gold or grain,
The cunning hand and cultured brain.

For well she keeps her ancient stock,
The stubborn strength of Pilgrim Rock;
And still maintains, with milder laws,
And clearer light, the Good Old Cause!

Nor heeds the sceptic's puny hands,
While near her school the church-spire stands;
Nor fears the blinded bigot's rule,
While near her church-spire stands the school!

EVENING IN BURMAH.[8]

A NIGHT of wonder! — piled afar
 With ebon feet and crests of snow,
Like Himalaya's peaks, which bar
The sunset and the sunset's star
 From half the shadowed vale below,
Volumed and vast the dense clouds lie,
And over them, and down the sky,
 Paled in the moon, the lightnings go.

And what a strength of light and shade
 Is chequering all the earth below! —
And, through the jungle's verdant braid,
Of tangled vine and wild reed made,
 What blossoms in the moonlight glow! —
The Indian rose's loveliness,
The ceiba with its crimson dress,
 The twining myrtle dropped with snow.

And flitting in the fragrant air,
  Or nestling in the shadowy trees,
A thousand bright-hued birds are there —
Strange plumage, quivering wild and rare,
  With every faintly breathing breeze;
And, wet with dew from roses shed,
The bulbul droops her weary head,
  Forgetful of her melodies.

Uprising from the orange-leaves,
  The tall pagoda's turrets glow;
O'er graceful shaft and fretted eaves,
Its verdant web the myrtle weaves,
  And hangs in flowering wreaths below;
And where the clustered palms eclipse
The moonbeams, from its marble lips
  The fountain's silver waters flow.

Strange beauty fills the earth and air,
  The fragrant grove and flowering tree,
And yet my thoughts are wandering where
My native rocks lie bleak and bare,

A weary way beyond the sea.
The yearning spirit is not here;
It lingers on a spot more dear
Than India's brightest bowers to me.

Methinks I tread the well-known street—
The tree my childhood loved is there,
Its bare-worn roots are at my feet,
And through its open boughs I meet
White glimpses of the place of prayer;
And unforgotten eyes again
Are glancing through the cottage pane,
Than Asia's lustrous eyes more fair.

O, holy haunts! oh, childhood's home!
Where, now, my wandering heart, is thine?
Here, where the dusky heathen come
To bow before the deaf and dumb,
Dead idols of their own design;
Where in the worshipped river's tide
The infant sinks, and on its side
The widow's funeral altars shine!

Here, where, mid light and song and flowers,
  The priceless soul in ruin lies —
Lost, dead to all those better powers
Which link this fallen world of ours
  To God's clear-shining Paradise;
And wrong and shame and hideous crime
Are like the foliage of their clime,
  The unshorn growth of centuries!

Turn, then, my heart; thy home is here;
  No other now remains for thee:
The smile of love, and friendship's tear,
The tones that melted on thine ear,
  The mutual thrill of sympathy,
The welcome of the household band,
The pressure of the lip and hand,
  Thou mayst not hear, nor feel, nor see.

God of my spirit! — Thou, alone,
  Who watchest o'er my pillowed head,
Whose ear is open to the moan
And sorrowing of thy child, hast known

The grief which at my heart has fed,—
The struggle of my soul to rise
Above its earth-born sympathies,—
The tears of many a sleepless bed!

O, be thine arm, as it hath been,
In every test of heart and faith,—
The tempter's doubt, the wiles of men,
The heathen's scoff, the bosom sin,—
A helper and a stay beneath;
A strength in weakness, through the strife
And anguish of my wasting life—
My solace and my hope, in death!

ALL'S WELL.

THE clouds, which rise with thunder, slake
  Our thirsty souls with rain;
The blow most dreaded falls to break
  From off our limbs a chain;
And wrongs of man to man but make
  The love of God more plain.
As through the shadowy lens of even
The eye looks farthest into heaven,
On gleams of star and depths of blue
The glaring sunshine never knew!

SEED TIME AND HARVEST.

As o'er his furrowed fields which lie
Beneath a coldly-dropping sky,
Yet chill with winter's melted snow,
The husbandman goes forth to sow;

Thus, Freedom, on the bitter blast
The ventures of thy seed we cast,
And trust to warmer sun and rain,
To swell the germ, and fill the grain.

Who calls thy glorious service hard?
Who deems it not its own reward?
Who, for its trials, counts it less
A cause of praise and thankfulness?

It may not be our lot to wield
The sickle in the ripened field;
Nor ours to hear, on summer eves,
The reaper's song among the sheaves;

Yet where our duty's task is wrought
In unison with God's great thought,
The near and future blend in one,
And whatsoe'er is willed is done!

And ours the grateful service whence
Comes, day by day, the recompense;
The hope, the trust, the purpose stayed,
The fountain and the noonday shade.

And were this life the utmost span,
The only end and aim of man,
Better the toil of fields like these
Than waking dream and slothful ease.

But life, though falling like our grain,
Like that revives and springs again;
And, early called, how blest are they
Who wait in heaven their harvest-day!

TO A. K.

ON RECEIVING A BASKET OF SEA MOSSES.

Thanks for thy gift
Of ocean flowers,
Born where the golden drift
Of the slant sunshine falls
Down the green, tremulous walls
Of water, to the cool, still coral bowers,
Where, under rainbows of perpetual showers,
God's gardens of the deep
His patient angels keep;
Gladdening the dim, strange solitude
With fairest forms and hues, and thus
Forever teaching us
The lesson which the many-colored skies,
The flowers, and leaves, and painted butterflies,
The deer's branched antlers, the gay bird that flings
The tropic sunshine from its golden wings,

The brightness of the human countenance,
Its play of smiles, the magic of a glance,
Forevermore repeat,
In varied tones and sweet,
That beauty, in and of itself, is good.

O, kind and generous friend, o'er whom
The sunset hues of Time are cast,
Painting, upon the overpast
And scattered clouds of noon-day sorrow,
The promise of a fairer morrow,
An earnest of the better life to come ;
The binding of the spirit broken,
The warning to the erring spoken,
The comfort of the sad,
The eye to see, the hand to cull
Of common things the beautiful,
The absent heart made glad
By simple gift or graceful token
Of love it needs as daily food,
All own one Source, and all are good !
Hence, tracking sunny cove and reach,
Where spent waves glimmer up the beach,

And toss their gifts of weed and shell
From foamy curve and combing swell,
No unbefitting task was thine
  To weave these flowers so soft and fair
In unison with His design,
  Who loveth beauty everywhere;
And makes in every zone and clime,
  In ocean and in upper air,
"All things beautiful in their time."

For not alone in tones of awe and power
    He speaks to man;
The cloudy horror of the thunder-shower
    His rainbows span;
    And, where the caravan
Winds o'er the desert, leaving, as in air
The crane-flock leaves, no trace of passage there,
    He gives the weary eye
The palm-leaf shadow for the hot noon hours,
    And on its branches dry
  Calls out the acacia's flowers;
  And, where the dark shaft pierces down

Beneath the mountain roots,
Seen by the miner's lamp alone,
The star-like crystal shoots;
So, where, the winds and waves below,
The coral-branchéd gardens grow,
His climbing weeds and mosses show,
Like foliage, on each stony bough,
Of varied hues more strangely gay
Than forest leaves in autumn's day;—
Thus evermore,
On sky, and wave, and shore,
An all-pervading beauty seems to say:
God's love and power are one; and they,
Who, like the thunder of a sultry day,
Smite to restore,
And they, who, like the gentle wind, uplift
The petals of the dew-wet flowers, and drift
Their perfume on the air,
Alike may serve Him, each, with their own gift,
Making their lives a prayer!

NOTES.

Note 1, page 6.

For the idea of this line, I am indebted to Emerson, in his inimitable sonnet to the Rhodora :

—— " If eyes were made for seeing,
Then Beauty is its own excuse for being."

Note 2, page 54.

Winnipiseogee : " Smile of the Great Spirit."

Note 3, page 70.

This legend is the subject of a celebrated picture by Tintoretto, of which Mr. Rogers possesses the original sketch. The slave lies on the ground, amid a crowd of spectators, who look on, animated by all the various emotions of sympathy, rage, terror ; a woman, in front, with a child in her arms, has always been admired for the lifelike vivacity of her attitude and expression. The executioner holds up the broken implements ; St. Mark, with a headlong movement, seems to rush down from heaven in haste to save his worshipper. The dramatic grouping in this picture is wonderful ; the coloring, in its gorgeous depth and harmony, is, in Mr. Rogers' sketch, finer than in the picture. — *Mrs. Jamieson's Poetry of Sacred and Legendary Art,* vol. 1, page 121.

Note 4, page 75.

Pennant, in his "Voyage to the Hebrides," describes the holy well of Loch Maree, the waters of which were supposed to effect a miraculous cure of melancholy, trouble, and insanity.

Note 5, page 85.

The writer of these lines is no enemy of Catholics. He has, on more than one occasion, exposed himself to the censures of his Protestant brethren, by his strenuous endeavors to procure indemnification for the owners of the convent destroyed near Boston. He defended the cause of the Irish patriots long before it had become popular in this country; and he was one of the first to urge the most liberal aid to the suffering and starving population of the Catholic island. The severity of his language finds its ample apology in the reluctant confession of one of the most eminent Romish priests, the eloquent and devoted Father Ventura.

Note 6, page 90.

Ebenezer Elliott, the intelligence of whose death has recently reached us, was, to the artisans of England, what Burns was to the peasantry of Scotland. His "Corn-law Rhymes" contributed not a little to that overwhelming tide of popular opinion and feeling which resulted in the repeal of the tax on bread. Well has the eloquent author of "The Reforms and Reformers of Great Britain" said of him — "Not corn-law repealers alone, but all Britons who moisten their scanty bread with the sweat of the brow, are largely indebted to his inspiring lays, for the mighty bound which the laboring mind of England has taken, in our day."

Note 7, page 95.

The reader of the Biography of the late William Allen, the philanthropic associate of Clarkson and Romilly, cannot fail to admire his simple and beautiful record of a tour through Europe, in the years 1818 and 1819, in the company of his American friend, Stephen Grellett.

Note 8, page 112.

It is an awful, an arduous thing, to root out every affection for earthly things, so as to live only for another world. I am now far, very far, from you all; but as often as I look around, and see the Indian scenery, I sigh to think of the distance tnat separates us. — *Letter of Henry Martyn from India.*

www.ingramcontent.com/pod-product-compliance
Lightning Source LLC
LaVergne TN
LVHW021420110826
845150LV00007B/2004